BECOMING THE PROVERBS 31 WOMAN

CHRISTINE MARIANA

Mariana Christine
Becoming the Proverbs 31 Woman
ISBN: 9798650775935

Contents

To God almighty for making this project a success

My spiritual parents Prophet and Prophetess Mary Bushiri. For the great teachings and support towards my life and above all spiritual growth.

My biological mother, Ms precious Milambo.

My godmother Dr. Jumoke Ayedele

My sister and her husband, Mr. and Mrs. Chilufya.

My friends and relatives, for believing in me and giving me strength and pushing me to be the beat in everything

To virtuous women Africa thank you ladies for believing I can be your source of strength.

And a huge thank you to my publisher for making this word a weapon of welfare and instrument of communication across the globe.

INTRODUCTION

I was only 15 years old when I started drinking and patronising night clubs. I did not see anything wrong with it. As long as I got drunk danced all night it was all that mattered. I struggled with peer pressure for 2 years I was disobedient to my mother and anyone else who ever tried to correct and lead me through the right path. My habits of sneaking out of the house became worse by the day; all I wanted was to be where there was music and alcohol, and to just be with my friends. I was one of a kind, I must say.

I remember one Christmas sneaking out of the house leaving my mother sleeping just so I could go and drink alcohol and have fun with my peers. I managed to go out but something happened that night, that changed me entirely. We were at my friends boarding house, and we decided to have a few bottles of alcohol before heading to the club. This was around 6pm when I'd only had two bottles I got so drunk and knocked out by those two bottles. This was so strange to me because I was a drunk and would drink over six bottles and still stand but on this fateful day only two bottles managed to knock me out.

After I had I passed out, my friends decided to leave me because according to them I was too drunk to even get ready for the club. The next morning, I woke up and found myself still at the boarding house. I was so furious that my friends had left me, so I decided to call them but no one would pick my calls. My conclusion was that I was being ignored, which made me really upset.

I interestingly received a phone call from my friend's number; however, I was very surprised to hear a man's voice. I wondered who it might've been.

"Maybe it's her boyfriend," I thought to myself, but it was actually a paramedic officer who was asking how I knew the owner of the phone. He then went on to asking me to call her mother because she had been involved in an accident.

In absolute shock, I quickly phoned my friend's mom and I passed on the message from the paramedic. I was very confused as to what had happened, so I decided to go to the hospital and actually see for myself.

I could not believe my eyes. The paramedic had lied to me, my friend had indeed gotten involved in an accident, but she had died on the spot.

The accident was very fatal, she was with two other of her friends she had gone with, and one died later that day and the other a week later.

To cut this long story short, God saved me from death and ironically I believe He used the very thing that I loved the most to save me, which was alcohol. That accident made me realise just how much God loved me; and everything that happened was just so I could see His glory and relevance in my life. It was after this incident that I gave my life fully to Christ and never looked back. I stopped going to the clubs, I stopped drinking alcohol and I stopped allowing things of this world influence me.

Having been raised by a single mother taught me a lot of things but the two most fundamental lessons were to be a prayer warrior and a survivor in this world we live in.

This world isn't for the faint hearted. As a young girl with big dreams I had to be strong and learn how to survive in this world - that seems like a jungle. Knowing fully well that all I had was God and my mother, in every step.

When I was 6 years old, we lived in an unfinished building after I lost my father Mr Rodgers Mbewe.

Growing up without a father is never easy, I would go to school on an empty stomach, I trekked to school

each day. This caused me a lot of emotional and mental trauma. The distance from home to school was very long and having to walk that distance on an empty stomach was never the easiest thing, not especially for a young girl like me.

One of my most difficult moments was when our school would host trips, but my mother could not afford to pay for me to go. My heart would break every time I saw my friends leave and I couldn't go.

Birthdays were the other event I dreaded. I would always wish that my father was alive just so he could buy me cake. I wanted to take it to school and celebrate with my friends, just like everyone else did in Junior Primary.

The pain of losing the pillar and joy of our household was vivid in my life as a little girl. I always looked at the roadside hoping to see my father come back home to us. I felt the pain of not having him in my life, not only as a father but a guide and a support system.

I had no one to look up to, not even my extended family were willing to help my mother with us and bills. I had to trust God. He was all I had. But as each day passed, I had to get ready and face the world head on. I knew that it would pay off someday.

For one I never imagined myself writing a book but God has consistently proven Himself victorious in my life.

He gifted me with intelligence, and that made me get noticed by people of high status in society. I became a young writer - with thanks to the Media Network on Child Rights and Development (MNCRD) — for all the knowledge I acquired during my time in the children news agency (CNA) which groomed me to the best of my abilities.

I received so much exposure and opportunities under the leadership of Mr. Henry Kabwe, Miss Prisca Sikana and Miss Consinivia Njobvu, I pray God blesses them ever so abundantly.

I love the proverb which says "it take a village to raise a child" I strongly agree with this because it did not take one person's effort for me to be where I am today. I believe it certainly took an entire village. This village includes people I had never imaged I would meet, and their influence contributed so much to the woman I have grown up to become and am still becoming.

When all seems to be crumbling down always remember that the Lord, God of Jacob is always by your side. It doesn't matter what was spoken against your life. Remember that He who began a good work in you shall surely finish it.

I may not know the struggle you are facing right now; whether it is loneliness, or whether it is the pain of losing that one person who was the pillar of your strength. Don't let that worry you because God is about to do a new thing in your life. I thought all hope was lost but God came through for me. He brought destiny helpers into my life and that made me whole again. He is about to do the same for you.

The bible in the book of Isaiah 43:19 says "see! I am doing a new thing! Now it springs forth do you not perceive it? I am making a way in the wilderness and streams in the Westland."

God knows you tried everything you knew to do but a time comes when you should trust Him to lead the way. Trusting God and not worrying about anything else.

If you believe this, just take a moment to shout a biggest "amen!" because it is done.

As you read this book, I believe God will begin to open your understanding to the things He is working out in your own life as well.

Amen.

FORGIVE YOUR PAST

CHAPTER 1

Many times we hold ourselves captive to our past. It could be a past filled with molestation that you encountered as a child, the loss of a loved one or maybe you witnessed a murder or you were kidnapped. But no matter what has happened to you in the past or what is happening to you right now, none of it has power to keep you from obtaining a great future.

John 3:16 says "for God so loved the world that He gave His only begotten Son that who so ever believes in Him should not perish but have everlasting life." See already this makes it easier for us to go to the Father because the reason He sent His Son is so that we could be pardoned of our iniquities. If you walk by faith in God, He will fulfil all of His promises over your life, you will live in victory and you will never be defeated.

Consider trees for a moment. As beautiful as trees are to look at, our natural eyes don't see what goes on underground as the trees grow from their roots. Trees must develop deep roots in order to grow strong and produce their beauty. We just see and enjoy the outward beauty, yet the same thing happens on the inside of us; like the roots of a tree, we are hard pressed on each side of life — in our well-being, careers, health, marriages, businesses, emotions and so on. But we carry on each day because there is always a drive and a hope for a better future.

It is our natural desire as humans to be happy and free from misery. We have to understand that the key to happiness is inner peace.

You may be wondering how to obtain inner peace. But the answer to that is pretty simple. It is by accepting Jesus as your Lord and personal Savior.

The greatest obstacles to inner peace are emotions such as anger, attachments, fear and suspicions, but all these are vanity because once you accept Jesus, there shouldn't be any reason to be angry or bitter do not dwell in your past any longer. 2 Corinthians 5:17   says "therefore, if anyone be in Christ Jesus the new creation has come, the old has gone the new is here."

Therefore, you do not stand a chance to keep holding on to the past that made you a bitter or resentful kind of person.

While love and compassion are a sense of universal responsibility, the commandment of our Lord Jesus Christ – which is love, becomes the real source of inner peace and happiness.

Refuse to be bitter. The whole point of forgiveness is to release the bad and the negative energy that flows through bitterness. When you have released the negativity around it, everything begins to flow freely and you begin to make better choices from a free spirit.

Romans 12:18-19 says "if it is possible, as far as it depends on you, live at peace with everyone. Do not take revenge, my dear friends, but leave room for God's wrath, for it is written: "It is mine to avenge; I will repay," says the Lord". You should know by this that everyone needs forgiveness and any consequences would naturally have been taken by God into His own hands, you do not need to keep holding on to any unforgiveness.

Our lives are governed by the choices we make and therefore it causes for us to be living in the consequences of our choices. However when you begin to forgive yourself, you find that the power of forgiveness releases you even from the effects of your choices and you can live freely all over again. Forgiveness dissolves the root of the unwanted patterns that persist in the lives we live. If everyone could forgive one another, we could all live in harmony.

It is imperative to infuse your life with action; don't just wait for things to happen.

Create your own future, create your happiness, create your own joy, create your own kind of love that you desire. So many times, people waiting for someone else to do that for them, when the reality is, you have power and ability to create your own reality...

It is important that you live a life in honor unto God, this is not by passively waiting for grace to come and work for you, but by doing what you can to make that grace a reality. Use the tools you have at your disposal, and better tools will be added along the way.

Forgive yourself for being imperfect, and for lusting after things of the flesh. It's hard to receive God's forgiveness and ultimately do the right thing when you're constantly condemning yourself.

Forgiving yourself gives you access to experiencing a life of holiness in God. Holiness is a process that requires for you to renew your mind. You have to allow yourself to go through the process that gives you the ability to be in complete control of your flesh.

The Bible says in Galatians 6:8 "he who sows in the flesh reaps in the flesh but he who sows in the spirit reaps in the spirit."

It's an entire process that requires you to replace things that stir up your flesh with things that stir up your spirit. For instance, you would have to replace movies with sermons, and to replace gossip with reading the word, you would have to replace flirting with random guys with praying in the spirit, and before you know it, you'd be experiencing evident spiritual growth.

God believes in you. I believe in you too. And I believe that God gave me this message for you because He truly believes in you. So, this is not about it being impossible. It is possible for you to be free of unforgiveness even from this moment henceforth.

Start by forgiving yourself for desiring to fornicate when you know you shouldn't. Forgive yourself for desiring just one glass of alcohol when you know you shouldn't be taking it. Forgive yourself for desiring to masturbate, watching porn or even just being tempted to have a whole outburst because of anger. Don't grow weary in trying to live holy. I understand that it is a lot of work, but I believe if you put in the work, you will reap a good reward!

SELF FORGIVENESS PRAYER

I thank you father for the power of forgiveness, I know Almighty God that you have forgiven me of all my sins. I thank you for your generous unconditional love and grace. Now dear Lord, I repent of my sins and ask that you help me overcome my shortcomings help me to forgive myself and to forgive those who have caused pain to my spirit in the name of Jesus Christ I pray amen.

LIVING YOUR PURPOSE

CHAPTER 2

I once heard a statement that says, "The two most important days in your life are the day you are born and the day you find out why." This is a powerful way to show that purpose is a very important aspect of anyone's life. However, so many people in life struggle with discovering their purpose, while others don't realise that they actually were created for a purpose. For one reason or another, they just can't seem to fully comprehend their reason for being called.

I have had people ask me what their purpose was and how to truly grab a hold of it.

According to dictionary.com, purpose is the reason for which something exists or is done made, used, etc. This means that when something is created, it has a cause, and I believe that by the time you finish reading this chapter, you would have an idea on why you were created. I believe you would have a clue into your purpose.

The weight of your worth is determined by the value you place upon yourself. You may have been the most hardworking, kindhearted, caring, humble, submissive and compassionate person ever, but in the midst of it all you lost track of your dignity, your identity or your purpose.

Your self-worth is not measured by your ability to survive neither is it measured by your ability to get things done. Self worth is the ability to see and value yourself rightly. How you perceive yourself determines the worth you carry.

It does not matter what people know or might hold against you, they don't have enough knowledge to create a weapon that can destroy you. The truth of the matter is that people around you will always have some negative things to say, and it is important that you do not pay attention to that. You determine your own worth.

There is always a constant battle between your spiritual and your reality. This is the part that you have to take care of your mind because your mind is a battle field where your purpose is either constructed or destroyed. The reality is always in constant conflict with the thoughts that you entertain in your mind. You have got to take care of your mind always because if you would allow yourself to let your mind be the devil's playground, you would not be able to fulfil your purpose if you are always running with what everyone is saying to you or about you.

When the enemy comes screaming at you don't be moved. You have to give your enemy the opportunity to scream whether it is a good or a bad report about your life. God Is the chief strategist, and what He usually does is that He uses that same enemy to send out the good news about you to the world around you. People will celebrate you at the voice of the enemy that tried to shame you. I always encourage that whenever you start feeling as though the enemy's voice has become too loud, you can take that as a rehearsal of him announcing your good news.

The bible says that God will prepare a table for you in front of your enemies. God will put your enemies to work for your own sake, God will make your enemies sweat for your benefit give them way. Psalm 23:5 "you prepare a table in the presence of my enemies. You anoint my head with oil; my cup overflows."

Never lose your identity and purpose because of temporary noises from the mouth of the devil. You are more than a conqueror

God saw it befitting that He blessed you with all the resources you need to live your purpose. Let's take a look at some of the most influential people of our generation; the likes of Prophet Shepherd Bushiri, Aliko Dangote, Sarah Jacks Roberts, etc.

One particular story I would like to focus on is the one of my spiritual father, Major Prophet Shepherd Bushiri. This story gives me so much hope and courage in God.

For Prophet Shepherd Bushiri, who was born in Malawi, which happens to be among the poorest countries in the world, he did not allow his environment to stop him. God still blessed and preserved him to being a great man of God that he is today. When we look at Major1's life today we can evidently see the hand of God over his life, despite all the battles he had to encounter, God always proved Himself victorious over our prophet's life. I believe he was also very determined to be better than how he grew up. I believe he was determined to do better and to be better, so he did not allow his circumstances to slow him down or to stop him. Imagination and determination can cause a drive in every young Christian's livelihood. Do not let anything stop you from archiving and living your purpose.

PRAYER OF PURPOSE

Heavenly Father I thank You that Your perfect plans and purposes can never be frustrated in my life and that You are working quietly in the background in order that Your divine will continues to progress towards its ultimate goal, as year succeeds to year.

I praise you that you have given me life and made me a new creation in Christ and thank You Father, that you have a special purpose for my life. Thank You that by Your grace, You are carrying out Your purposes in the lives of all Your children - that Christ is all and in all and I pray that this may be realised in my life as well.

I pray that You would equip me and enable me to fulfil the plan and purpose that you have for me. I ask that You use every gift and talent that You have graciously given to me, to Your praise and glory. Help me to fulfil all that You would have me do in my life and give me grace to be obedient to Your voice as I seek to carry out Your purpose for my life. May I rejoice evermore and pray without ceasing.

Teach me to give thanks in all things and hearken to the voice of Your Holy Spirit and may I hold fast to that which is good and abstain from all forms of evil – knowing that this is Your will for my life... in Jesus name I pray, AMEN.

YOUR GOING-THROUGH IS NOT YOUR GOING-TO

CHAPTER 3

Until you manifest the glory of God that is on the inside of you, it is not over. The book of Genesis chapter 38, narrates the story of Judah and Tamar – the name Tamar means palm tree. Palm trees naturally hold a very important significance in humanity, the bible talks about palm trees as trees that flourish very well and are always well watered in the dry land, however; it was not so in Tamar's life.

Take a look at Tamar's story:

It came to pass at that time that Judah departed from his brothers, and visited a certain Adullamite whose name was Hirah. 2 And Judah saw there a daughter of a certain Canaanite whose name was Shua, and he married her and went in to her. **3** *So she conceived and bore a son, and he called his name Er.* **4** *She conceived again and bore a son, and she called his name Onan.* **5** *And she conceived yet again and bore a son, and called his name Shelah. He was at Chezib when she bore him.*

6 *Then Judah took a wife for Er his firstborn, and her name was Tamar.* **7** *But Er, Judah's firstborn, was wicked in the sight of the Lord, and the Lord killed him.* **8** *And Judah said to Onan, "Go in to your brother's wife and marry her, and raise up an heir to your brother."* **9** *But Onan knew that the heir would not be his; and it came to pass, when he went in to his brother's wife, that he emitted on the ground, lest he should give an heir to his brother.* **10** *And the thing which he did [a]displeased the Lord; therefore He killed him also.*

11 *Then Judah said to Tamar his daughter-in-law, "Remain a widow in your father's house till my son Shelah is grown." For he said, "Lest he also die like his brothers." And Tamar went and dwelt in her father's house.*

12 *Now in the process of time the daughter of Shua, Judah's wife, died; and Judah was comforted, and went up to his sheepshearers at Timnah, he and his friend Hirah the*

Adullamite. ¹³ And it was told Tamar, saying, "Look, your father-in-law is going up to Timnah to shear his sheep." ¹⁴ So she took off her widow's garments, covered herself with a veil and wrapped herself, and sat in an open place which was on the way to Timnah; for she saw that Shelah was grown, and she was not given to him as a wife. ¹⁵ When Judah saw her, he thought she was a harlot, because she had covered her face. ¹⁶ Then he turned to her by the way, and said, "Please let me come into you"; for he did not know that she was his daughter-in-law.

So, she said, "What will you give me, that you may come into me?"

¹⁷ And he said, "I will send a young goat from the flock."

So, she said, "Will you give me a pledge till you send it?"

¹⁸ Then he said, "What pledge shall I give you?"

So, she said, "Your signet and cord, and your staff that is in your hand." Then he gave them to her, and went into her, and she conceived by him. ¹⁹ So she arose and went away and laid aside her veil and put on the garments of her widowhood.

20 *And Judah sent the young goat by the hand of his friend the Adullamite, to receive his pledge from the woman's hand, but he did not find her.* 21 *Then he asked the men of that place, saying, "Where is the harlot who was openly by the roadside?"*

And they said, "There was no harlot in this place."

22 *So he returned to Judah and said, "I cannot find her. Also, the men of the place said there was no harlot in this place."*

23 *Then Judah said, "Let her take them for herself, lest we be shamed; for I sent this young goat and you have not found her."*

24 *And it came to pass, about three months after, that Judah was told, saying, "Tamar your daughter-in-law has played the harlot; furthermore she is [c]with child by harlotry."*

So, Judah said, "Bring her out and let her be burned!"

25 *When she was brought out, she sent to her father-in-law, saying, "By the man to whom these belong, I am with child." And she said, "Please determine whose these are— the signet and cord, and staff."*

²⁶ So Judah acknowledged them and said, "She has been more righteous than I, because I did not give her to Shelah my son." And he never knew her again.

²⁷ Now it came to pass, at the time for giving birth, that behold, twins were in her womb. ²⁸ And so it was, when she was giving birth, that the one put out his hand; and the midwife took a scarlet thread and bound it on his hand, saying, "This one came out first." ²⁹ Then it happened, as he drew back his hand, that his brother came out unexpectedly; and she said, "How did you break through? This breach be upon you!" Therefore his name was called Perez. ³⁰ Afterward his brother came out who had the scarlet thread on his hand. And his name was called Zerah.

Genesis 38:1-30

Isn't it something to marvel about, that Tamar was the first woman mentioned in Matthew's explanation of Jesus' genealogy (Matthew 1). Tamar's story is one of desperation that was born of shattered hope. She was the daughter-in-law of Judah – the son of Jacob. Tamar was married to two of Judah's sons, both of whom were bad and died under the judgement of the Lord.

After they died, Judah then promised to give her to his youngest son once he'd come of age. The reality is that Judah never intended to keep that promise. He hoped that Tamar would eventually just go away before his son had matured enough.

However; in a world where women received no respect if they were not married and with children, Tamar was left in a desperate situation. She decided to take matters into her own hands by disguising herself as a prostitute, and she slept with her father-in-law – Judah, and bore him twin sons. One of the twins, whom she named Perez, would later become a direct forefather of Jesus Christ.

Once the sordid affair came to light, Judah publicly admitted that Tamar was more righteous than he was. Which was an accurate assessment given his cruel, callous treatment towards her.

While Tamar's actions aren't justifiable either, they're certainly understandable.Tamar was indeed a complicated person with a messy life.

This story is evidence of God's merciful attribute. Through Tamar, God showed His mercy by allowing Jesus to come through that very bloodline. This is not to condone uncanny behaviour, but it shows that God can be merciful in desperate situations.

WHEN GOD WANTS TO COME BIG, HE COMES LATE.

God gave Tamar double for her trouble.

There are so many times we face challenges, and we feel as though God cannot see what we are going through, but the truth is that God is all knowing, He sees everything and He knows how to turn any situation to work together for your good.

In the same way Tamar's dignity was restored, I believe God can restore your lost dignity as well in the name of Jesus Christ.

"I will open rivers in high places, and fountains in the midst of the valleys: I will make the wilderness a pool of water, and the dry land springs of water. I will plant in the wilderness the cedar, the Shittah tree, and the myrtle, and the oil tree; I will set in the desert the fir tree, and the pine, and the box tree together: That they may see, and know, and consider, and understand together, that the hand of the

PRAYER OF RESTORATION

Heavenly Father, I know I have wasted so many years of my life pursuing the wrong things and getting involved with worldly activities, fleshly pursuits, while neglecting the important spiritual issues, which are eternal and lasting. I ask for Your forgiveness, and I pray that by Your mercy, You would restore to me the years that the locusts have eaten the years that I have foolishly wasted.

Lord, I want to be a good and faithful servant when I stand before Your throne, and I know that most if not all of the good works I have done are likely to be burned up, knowing that I have been striving in the flesh instead of resting in You and letting Your Holy Spirit live and work through me. Restore to me the heavenly joy and inner peace that has been evading me... help me to focus on the eternal rather than the temporal and from this day forward, may I start to live my life in a way that you would have me live, in the mighty name of Jesus I pray,

Amen.

YOUR CONFIDENCE

CHAPTER 5

God is a confident God, and you are His offspring, which therefore means you are expected to be a confident child of God. If you are confident, you cannot be a carrier of worry.

Our confidence is usually challenged by a life of low esteem towards self. This is what is known as having a low self-esteem. Many people might confuse their esteem of self as humility, but that is not so. The word of God calls us to living our lives in a humble way, and while that is great, you have to understand that being humble is not thinking lowly of yourself.

Humility is when you think about yourself less than you think about other people, while insecurity is thinking of yourself all the time. The irony about having a low self-esteem is that, it could be a form of pride, because; a person with low self-esteem considers themselves to be worth very little, but they're still thinking about themselves more than they think of others.

A person with a low self-esteem is one who considers themselves to be worth very little. But the factors on which you come to that conclusion are usually based off of what the standard of the world. The way the world standardises things. Unfortunately, according to the standard of the world, you can never really match up, no matter how perfect you may be.

There are several things that the world bases worth on, and these are:

* The way you look
* How much you weigh
* The amount in your bank account
* The clothes or brands you own
* Where you work or what you do
* How many followers you have?
* Who you know?
* Your status quo …

The list goes on and on. However, as Christians, those are things you should not be looking at. Our standards are not and should never be measured by the world.

We should always see things from the lenses of God's eyes. The moment you understand what God sees when He looks at you, you will begin to be confident in yourself.

You were made in the image of God, and God is valuable, therefore you have value. God Himself sees you as valuable and that is why He sent Jesus Christ – His Son, to die on the cross in your place, so that God could be reconciled to you and have relationship with you.

Proverbs 23:7 says 'For as he thinks in his heart, so is he. "Eat and drink!" he says to you, But his heart is not with you."

Therefore, you cannot expect to be anything more than the limits you place in your own mind. The limit is in your mind, for as you think, so are you.

When you change the quality of your thinking, you change the quality of your life. You can decide how you will focus your thoughts in any given situation. Your thoughts and feelings determine your actions and your actions determine the results you get. It all starts with your thinking.

I understand the mind is a battlefield and that is absolutely normal for all humans, which is why you should constantly speak the word of God over yourself daily to remind you of your identity. Take time to write down affirmations and always keep them handy, because moments will come when you will feel lost and low, but those affirmations will be a reminder to yourself about who you are. Consistently speaking positively about yourself, to yourself, is a great way to start growing in confidence and keeping a lighter mood always.

DAILY AFFIRMATIONS

* I am becoming a better version of myself every day, and I am proud of my achievements.
* I love who I am right now, because this is exactly who God created me to be.
* I will not stop working hard
* I am patient

* I am everything God says I am

* I do everything in the spirit of excellence.

* I speak only in love because I understand that there is power in the tongue

* I am not a failure; one event of failure does not conclude who I am.

* I have people I can depend on for help, so I will not try to do everything on my own.

* God does not compare me to other people. I am unique in my own way.

* I will not try to help God do His work in me, I will trust the process and the journey that He has placed me on.

PRAYER FOR CONFIDENCE

Heavenly Father, I ask that You may help me build up my confidence. While I grow in confidence, I pray that you help me to remain humble. Teach me to have courage in all I do, so that I may be able to minister your word and walk in what I believe in, without being afraid. I pray that you cause me to burn like a fire, and let that fire spread in a form of love into the lives of others. In the mighty name of Jesus Christ.

THE LOVE AFFAIR

CHAPTER 6

Love is a beautiful thing to experience. Unfortunately many times we fall prey to actions that seem to us as love. Men define love totally different to the way that women define it as, and sometimes people confuse love with infatuation or affection. The differences between these are that love is a profoundly tender, passionate affection for another, while affection is the fondness and or state of mind that is often associated with feeling. Infatuation on the other hand is defined as the state of being carried away by an unreasoned passion towards another person whom you have developed strong romantic feelings for.

Our inability to differentiate these is what makes many fall into the wrong trap, under the assumption that it was love.

In this chapter, my hope is to get you to an understanding of the reality of love, how you can identify it from within you and from others. This would help you to not become a constant victim of heartbreaks all the time.

As a woman, it is important to learn yourself and have value over your own emotions. This is it just for the single women, so if you are married, you are also included in this. From a place of wisdom, and from a place of understanding, I would like to take this time to break some things down.

The fundamental state of marriage should be based on love and respect, this is according to Ephesians 5:33.

The bible clearly states that women should respect their husbands, while husbands love their wives. It is unfortunate that many women do not have respect for their husbands because the husbands do not show love to their wives. This instruction is reciprocal, so in the same way, some men do not show love to their wives because they feel as though their wives do not respect them enough.

The reason is usually because of lack of communication and lack of understanding between the partners. Sometimes the foundation of the relationship is the major reason for a later fall, especially in this aspect.

Marriage is an important aspect of a believer, and therefore you cannot just divorce your spouse in the name of having misunderstood each other. This is why it is important to take inventory of your feelings towards each other before you get married.

1 Corinthians 7:10-11 says "To the married I give this charge [not I, but the Lord): the wife should not separate from her husband (but if she does, she should remain unmarried or else be reconciled to her husband), and the husband should not divorce his wife."

From that we see that God is against divorce so it should never be a solution.

The bible proves some secrets to happy marriages, below are some you may learn from.

Who[c] can find a [d]virtuous wife?

For her worth is far above rubies.

11 The heart of her husband safely trusts her;

So he will have no lack of gain.

12 She does him good and not evil

All the days of her life.

13 She seeks wool and flax,

And willingly works with her hands.

14 She is like the merchant ships,

She brings her food from afar.

15 She also rises while it is yet night,

And provides food for her household,

And a portion for her maidservants.

16 She considers a field and buys it;

From [c]her profits she plants a vineyard.

17 She girds herself with strength,

And strengthens her arms.

18 She perceives that her merchandise is good,

And her lamp does not go out by night.

19 She stretches out her hands to the distaff,

And her hand holds the spindle.

20 She extends her hand to the poor,

Yes, she reaches out her hands to the needy.

21 She is not afraid of snow for her household,

For all her household is clothed with scarlet.

22 She makes tapestry for herself;

Her clothing is fine linen and purple.

23 Her husband is known in the gates,

When he sits among the elders of the land.

24 She makes linen garments and sells them,

And supplies sashes for the merchants.

25 Strength and honour are her clothing;

She shall rejoice in time to come.

26 She opens her mouth with wisdom,

And on her tongue is the law of kindness.

27 She watches over the ways of her household,

And does not eat the bread of idleness.

28 Her children rise up and call her blessed;

Her husband also, and he praises her:

29 "Many daughters have done well,

But you excel them all."

30 Charm is deceitful and beauty is passing,

But a woman who fears the Lord, she shall be praised.

31 Give her of the fruit of her hands,

And let her own works praise her in the gates.

Proverbs 31:10-31

These scriptures still apply even to the modern-day wife, or soon to be wife. So, we cannot say that this does not apply to today's world. While a lot of things have changed, the principles of God's word have not changed. In order for your marriage to work you will need to follow a few guidelines on principles of being a godly wife a wife of noble character in a modern world.

Always remember that weddings are not marriages. Therefore, more investment must be made in the marriage aspect and not only just the wedding.

It is important for the single woman, and for the wife to learn to be faithful to themselves and to their spouses. Being a woman of integrity is a non-negotiable, you have to be mindful of how you carry yourself, the way you talk and walk. The way you respond to situations around you. Your integrity will be your best weapon.

A woman should have self-respect, that means you should not be easily accessible to anyone. Always remember you are a wife before you try to befriend anyone, therefore, carry yourself as such.

For the married women, it is very important that you do not disclose your marital problems to your friends or to your relatives. You have got to not trust everyone else with your marriage issues other than God. It is important to have a marriage mentor who is actually successful in their own marriage as well.

Make it a point to always take care of your skin, your hair, brushing your teeth always. Make yourself always look presentable, even if you are married, it is important that you do so.

It is very important that you train yourself to be calm at all times. Your mouth should produce words of life, not death or destruction. This means that if there is anything that might bother you for any reason, it is important that you teach yourself to be calm before you respond or react to the situation.

Appreciate Your Man

To appreciate him means to set a value on him, to raise him to a great standard of his full worth, and to appreciate him for all he does for you.

You may learn to show your appreciation on three main ways which are:

*Choose not to focus on his faults.

•Let him take the lead, and you take the submission cap. Do not be nagging, the bible even says there's nothing worse than a nagging wife. Appreciate him when he does nice things, whether big or small.

•Look at him with the eyes of love. Show him that you are confident of him as a man and that you feel safe around him. Men love those kinds of affirmations.

For some women it is very difficult to submit to their husbands because they feel as though their husband's ego's stand in the way. That feeling may be awful, but you can always take a leap of faith and appreciate who he was when you met him, the kindness and intelligence that he portrays and so on.

A German author by the name Goethe once wrote "if you treat a man as he is, he will stay as he is, but if you treat him as he were what he ought to be and could be, he would he will become that bigger and better man."

When you have an unwavering faith in his better side, you inspire him to live up to your conception of his ability. You offer him hope and eventually he begins to change.

I want you to experience a good marriage in Jesus name.

Prayer for A Happy Marriage

Heavenly Father, I thank You for your grace towards me and for giving me the spouse that You gave me, I ask that You may strengthen our bond of unity in our marriage, I understand that a threefold cord cannot easily be broken so I ask that You may always be our guide in our marriage so that we may know how to handle issues, because of Your presence. I ask that you enable us to be united and ensure that nothing will come between us. I ask for the wisdom to identify and work through anything that is not pleasing to you in our marriage, whether that be spiritually, physically or emotionally.

I am excited to seeing the work of your hand as we do our best to seek your face daily. Thank you for these blessings and many others. In Jesus Name.

Amen.

Single and Happy

Single-hood is not a curse, however most people often miss out on enjoying their time while they're single. The need for validation from another constantly stands in the way, and it causes us to not be in touch with our emotions. The issue with emotions is that we end up falling for the wrong type of people and that brings a bad end to the relationship.

While in your single season, there are things I would like you to note and work on in your life.

❖ ARE YOU WHOLE?

Wholeness is an important aspect that you should be working on while you wait on your future spouse. To be whole, you have to address the issues of the heart. You have to release yourself from past pains, and be yourself in the present. Once you live in the present and can connect with the true reality of your present moment, you will be able to align and restore your heart. When your heart begins to heal and be restored, it becomes easier to trust your heart to lead you, and to discern the good ones from the bad, because you would not be choosing from a place of desperation.

You can easily become a loving, joyful person who is full of peace with the power and authority to forgive and forget and bless those all around you.

You become a healthy person even for those around you if you choose to take inventory of your pain and begin to work on it while you are still single. If you still hold on to your past pain and grudges, that is a sure sign that you have not healed from that and you are not whole.

❖ BE HAPPY WITH YOURSELF.

Happiness is a sense of well-being, joy, or contentment. It is important to evaluate whether or not you are happy with yourself. Remember that the principle of life is that you cannot give what you do not have. You cannot give what you don't have. Always remember that you cannot be happy with anyone if you are not happy with yourself, You cannot expect to be happy in a relationship if you were never happy while you were single. Therefore embrace your singleness. Learn to make yourself happy while you are still single. Consider it all joy when you are in your single season; because it is in your singleness that God creates purpose. It is when you are in your single season that God births and cultivates new gifts and talents. When you are in that season, it is your time to discover who you truly are.

Being single can be very lonely and difficult. You would have to go to weddings alone, and that can be depressing. You may have issues with your car and not have anyone to help you with it, and that could be frustrating. But when you look at it and you realise that you rushed for a relationship, and you put your heart on the line, then having it shattered to pieces would be worse than just having waited.

So, if you could look at it from a different perspective, then you would cause yourself to see single-hood from a different perspective. You could begin to enjoy your single-hood.

It is in your single season that you can really do what you like, freely. You get to spend time with your friends, you travel the world, as far as you want to. As far as you choose to. In your single season, you schedule your time in a way that is convenient for you.

Above all, you can be sure to spend time with the Lord, uninterrupted. You get to learn more in the word of God. You get to take your time growing spiritually. You can serve God fully and nothing will stop you or pull you back.

❖ Trust in God

You need to train yourself to trust God at all times. David understood this concept. He trusted God to deliver him from his enemies and those that pursued to end his life. God delivered him and provided food in the desert; He gave him companions and homes; even comforted him when he was down.

David wrote by experience, "Those who know your name will trust in you, for you, Lord have never forsaken those who seek you." (Ps 9:10) When you go through tough times, or you have needs or anything that threatened your natural comfort, you have to trust God to come through for you. God can rescue you from wrong relationships, He can save you for the right one. HE is good!

He can be trusted to provide and protect to comfort and to heal you. Knowing God can be trusted should give you a sense of peace and wonderful freedom to do all He asks with a joyful heart even while you are still single.

❖ Intimacy with God

We all are created for intimacy. To be fully known and to fully know Him. We were created to be loved as well as to fully love. Our hearts are created to be filled only with the love of God, outside of which, we are voice from deep within. We seek it. We crave it. We do crazy things for it, but only intimacy with God can fill those voids. God longs for intimacy with us.

The Book of Songs of Solomon in the Bible is a love story of how God pursues relationship with us. How delighted He is when we respond to His call and how totally content and secure we can become in His love.

When you begin to seek God; to know Him, what He likes, His dislikes, sorrows and joys, you will understand the essence of true intimacy with God. He speaks to you and He is with you at all times. You will know true love. Jesus becomes dearer than life itself and walking through each day with Him becomes pure delight.

Your desires and pursuits change to be in line with His. One thing you need to desire is purity because it is the pure in heart that will see God, according to Matt 5: 8

❖ PURSUING PURITY

The Apostle Paul said a lot about purity. He admonished us to "flee from sexual immorality" which is a sin against your body, the temple of the Holy Spirit (I Cor. 6:18). Instead "purify us from everything that contaminates body and spirit, perfecting holiness out of reverence for God."

Purity is possible, and it is still required of us, even in this generation. I know, by God's grace that even if you have already given yourself to a man you can still practice purity while you wait for your God ordained husband. God provides a way out of every temptation, it is your responsibility to grab the escape route and run with it. God gives strength to overcome sexual desires, call on Jesus when you ache for sexual intimacy. A life of purity eliminates the fears of STD's, AIDS, pregnancy and all their complications. If you observe the hurt, pain and devastation that comes from sex outside marriage, you would be asking God for wisdom to truly help you wait. This is not just theory, it is reality

Purity also has a spiritual aspect. You have to guard your eyes against what you watch, and you have to set a guard against what you listen to. You can be a positive influencer by bringing purity to conversations and gatherings rather than being influenced to compromise.

Don't give the devil the entrance into your thoughts. Set your mind on things above. The beauty of life is revealed in staying focused on God. Desire to be the woman described in Proverbs 31.

Your single season is a time of preparation for marriage and a greater calling that God has for you.

Marriage is not the goal, however, is the wheel which carries you to the fullness of the call of God on your life.

NUGGETS

❖ You are a queen and as such you need to set some boundaries in your life.

❖ Learn from your past mistakes

❖ Build yourself (HOW) and discover your likes and dislikes

❖ Dress decently

❖ Understand that dating will not change your entire life therefore do not look for someone else to complete you, that is your personal responsibility to be whole.

❖ Enjoy your life to the fullest.

❖ Spend some time dating yourself,

❖ Take yourself out to dinner,

❖ Learn to enjoy your own company.

❖ Keep an open mind.

❖ Being single doesn't mean that anything is wrong with you. Being single is not a deformity

❖ Believe that God has a great person for you that He is preparing for you; all you have to do is trust Him.

❖ Respect yourself in all areas, talking, dressing, lifestyle.

SINGLE'S PRAYER

Dear Lord God, thank you for loving me so deeply. Thank You for loving me even when I was so far, caught up in my selfish thoughts and desires. King of glory, please help me seek Your face in all I do. May I cultivate an intimate and meaningful relationship with You and live a life that is poured-out for Your glory? Thank You for reminding me that my singleness does not change Your love or plans for me in Jesus name. I pray this day to remain committed to you and as your dear Son, my Savior Jesus Christ, did, to continually pray "not my will but yours be done". In the mighty name of Jesus Christ, I pray, Amen.

ABOUT THE AUTHOR

Christine Mariana is a young and passion driven Christian influencer. She is the founder and President of The Virtuous Women Africa, which is a women empowerment movement (VWA). The VWA movement has thousands of followers all around the world. Christine runs a philanthropy drive under this movement.

Christine She is also Director and CEO of Kazon Group of Companies based in South Africa and Zambia.

www.ingramcontent.com/pod-product-compliance
Lightning Source LLC
Chambersburg PA
CBHW051358150726
48000CB00003B/1240